Parenting
Without the
Power Struggles

FOSTER CLINE, MD
& JIM FAY

Parenting
Without the
Power Struggles

NAVPRESS

*A NavPress resource published in alliance
with Tyndale House Publishers, Inc.*

NavPress is the publishing ministry of The Navigators, an international Christian organization and leader in personal spiritual development. NavPress is committed to helping people grow spiritually and enjoy lives of meaning and hope through personal and group resources that are biblically rooted, culturally relevant, and highly practical.

For more information, visit www.NavPress.com.

21	20	19	18	17	16	15
8	7	6	5	4	3	2

Contents

Parenting: Joy or Nightmare?   7
Are We Having Fun Yet?
Putting the Fun Back into Parenting

Mission Possible: Raising Responsible Kids   15
Ineffective Parenting Styles
The Effective Parenting Style of Love and Logic
To Protect Them Is Not to Love Them
Responsibility Cannot Be Taught

Responsible Children Feel Good about Themselves   31
I Am What I Think You Think I Am
Positive Self-Esteem Comes from Accomplishment
If We're Happy, They're Happy

Children's Mistakes Are Their Opportunities   45
You Have Your Troubles, I Have Mine
The Two Rules of Love and Logic

It's Never Too Late to Start   59

Notes   61

About the Authors   63

Parenting:
Joy or Nightmare?

A wise child loves discipline,
but a scoffer does not listen to rebuke.

PROVERBS 13:1

A mother and father stand outside of a restaurant in the rain asking their three-year-old, Chloe, to get in the car so the family can go home. Chloe refuses. Her parents spend the next fifteen minutes begging and pleading with her to do it on her own. At one point, the father gets down on his knees in the puddles, trying to reason her into the car. She finally complies, but only after her parents agree to buy her a soda on the way home. If they have to use a soda to buy her off at three, what will they be facing when she reaches sixteen?

• • •

Jim sits in the airport awaiting a flight, watching as a mother gives at least eighty different demands to her three-year-old boy over the course of an hour without ever enforcing one of them:

"Come back here, Logan!"

"You better listen to me, Logan, or else!"

"I mean it, Logan!"

"Don't run, Logan!"

Logan eventually finds his way to where Jim is seated. The toddler smiles at him while ignoring his mother. The mother yells, "Logan, you get away from that man! You get over here this instant!"

Jim smiles down at Logan and asks, "Hey, Logan, what is your mom going to do if you don't get over there?"

He looks up and grins. "She not goin' to do nothin'." And then his eyes twinkle and his grin becomes wider.

It turns out he is right. She finally comes apologizing. "I'm sorry he's bothering you, but you know how three-year-olds are. They just won't listen to one thing you tell them."

• • •

On a Saturday at a local supermarket, two boys, ages five and seven, have declared war. Like guerrillas on a raid, they sneak from aisle to aisle, hiding behind displays and squeaking their tennies on the tile floor. Then suddenly a crash—the result of a game of "shopping cart chicken"—pierces the otherwise calming background Muzak.

The mother, having lost sight of this self-appointed commando unit, abandons her half-filled cart. As she rounds a corner, her screams turn the heads of other shoppers: "Don't touch that! *You*—get over here!" She races for the boys, and as she's about to grab two sweaty necks, they turn to Tactic B: the "split-up," a twenty-first-century version of "divide and conquer." Now she must run in two directions at once to shout at them. Wheezing with exertion, she corrals the younger one, who has just blitzed the cereal section, leaving a trail of boxes. But when she returns him to her cart, the older boy is gone. She locates him in produce, rolling seedless grapes like marbles across the floor.

After scooping up boy number two and carrying him back—you guessed it—she finds that boy number one has disappeared. Mom sprints from her cart once more. Finally, after she threatens murder and the pawning of their Nintendo game system, the boys are gathered.

But the battle's not over. Tactic C follows: the "fill the cart when Mom's not looking" game. Soon M&M's, Oreos, vanilla wafers, and jumbo Snickers bars are piled high. Mom races back and forth, reshelving the treats. Then come boyish smirks and another round of threats from Mom: "Don't do that! I'm going to slap your hands!" And in a cry of desperation: "You're never going to leave the house again for the rest of your lives!"

Frazzled, harried, and broken, Mom finally surrenders and buys off her precious flesh and blood with candy bars—a cease-fire that guarantees enough peace to finish her rounds.

Are We Having Fun Yet?

Ah yes, parenting—the joys, the rewards. We become parents with optimism oozing from every pore. During late-night feedings and sickening diaper changes, we know we are laying the groundwork for a lifelong relationship that will bless us when our hair turns gray or disappears. We look forward to times of tenderness and times of love, shared joys and shared disappointments, hugs and encouragement, words of comfort and soul-filled conversations.

But the joys of parenting were far from the minds of the parents in the previous stories. No freshly scrubbed cherubs flitted through their lives, hanging on every soft word dropping from Mommy's or Daddy's lips. Where was that gratifying, loving, personal relationship between parent and child? The sublime joys of parenting were obliterated by a more immediate concern: survival.

This was parenting, the nightmare.

Scenes like these happen to the best of us. When they do, we may want to throw our hands in the air and scream, "Kids! Are they worth the pain?" Sometimes kids can be a bigger hassle than a house with one shower. When we think of the enormous love we pump into our children's lives and then the sassy, disobedient, unappreciative behavior we receive in return, we can get pretty burned out on the whole process. Besides riddling our lives with day-to-day hassles, kids present us with perhaps the greatest challenge of our adulthood: raising our children to be responsible adults.

Through the miracle of birth, we are given a

tiny, defenseless babe totally dependent on us for every physical need. We have a mere eighteen years at most to ready that suckling for a world that can be cruel and heartless. That child's success in the real world hinges in large part on the job we do as parents. Just thinking about raising responsible, well-rounded kids sends a sobering shiver of responsibility right up the old parental spine. Many of us have felt queasy after a thought such as: *If I can't handle a five-year-old in a grocery store, what am I going to do with a fifteen-year-old who seems to have an enormous understanding of sex and is counting the days until he gets a driver's license?*

Putting the Fun Back into Parenting

All is not so bleak. Trust us! There's hope shining beacon bright at the end of the tunnel of parental frustration. Parenting doesn't have to be drudgery. Children can grow to be thinking, responsible adults. We can help them do it without living through an eighteen-year horror movie.

The approach we've found to have proven success is what we call "Parenting with Love and Logic." It's a win-win philosophy that is all about raising responsible kids. Parents win because they love in a healthy way and establish control over their kids without resorting to the anger and threats that encourage rebellious teenage behavior. Kids win because they learn responsibility and the logic of life by solving their own problems. Thus, they acquire the tools for coping with the real world.

Parents and kids can establish a rewarding relationship built on love and trust in the process. What a deal! By parenting with Love and Logic you can do away with power struggles and put the fun back into parenting.[1]

Mission Possible:
Raising Responsible Kids

Train children in the right way,
and when old, they will not stray.

PROVERBS 22:6

All loving parents face essentially the same challenge: raising children who have their heads on straight and will have a good chance to make it in the big world. Every sincere mom and dad strives to attain this goal. We must equip our darling offspring to make the move from total dependence on us to independence, from being controlled by us to controlling themselves.

Let's face it: In this incredibly complex, fast-changing age, only responsible kids will be able to handle the real world that awaits them. Life-and-death decisions confront teenagers—and even younger children—at every turn. Many of the temptations of adult life—drugs, Internet pornography, premarital sex, alcohol—are thrown at kids every day. The statistics on teen depression and suicide bear out the seriousness of the parental task. How will our children handle such intense pressures? What choices will they make when faced with these life-and-death decisions? What will they do when we are no longer pouring wise words into their ears? Will merely telling them to be responsible get the job done? These are the questions that should guide the development of our parenting philosophy.

The gravity of the parenting task hit home some years ago when my (Jim's) son, Charlie, was a teenager. Charlie asked to use the family car to go to a party. "It's the party of the year," Charlie said. "Everybody who's anybody will be there."

I trusted Charlie and would have loaned him the car, but I had a speaking engagement the same evening and couldn't oblige. Charlie's mother, Shirley, had plans of her own for the second car.

"Why don't you hitch a ride with Randy?" I suggested, referring to Charlie's best friend.

Charlie shook his head. "That's okay. I understand. I guess I won't go." Then he went to his room. I knew something was up. This was *the* party of the year, so I talked to Charlie and pried loose some more information. Randy, it seemed, had started drinking at parties, and Charlie decided he'd rather stay home than risk the danger of riding with a friend who was likely to drink and drive.

The night of that party, Randy, plastered with booze, drove himself and five passengers off the side of a mountain at eighty miles per hour.

Today, roughly two decades later, Charlie has earned his PhD and is on staff at the Love and Logic Institute. He is now teaching others the same parenting techniques that saved his life. Because he had learned to be a responsible teen, instead of dying that night he has gone on to help countless others.

Unfortunately, many kids arrive at their challenging and life-threatening teenage years with no clue how to make decisions. They "know better" but still try drugs. They ignore good advice from parents and other adults and dabble with sex. Despite warnings to be cautious, they are still lured into meetings by Internet predators. Why do young people sometimes seem so stupidly self-destructive? The tragic truth is that many of these foolish choices are the first real decisions they have ever made. In childhood, decisions were always made for them by well-meaning parents. We must understand that making good choices is like any other activity: It has to be learned. The teenagers who make the wrong choice on alcohol are probably the same children who never learned how to keep their hands out of the cookie jar.

Parents who take their parenting job seriously want to raise responsible kids, kids who at any age can confront the important decisions of their lives with maturity and good sense. Good parents learn to do what is best for their children. Those little tykes, so innocent and playful, will someday grow up. We want to do everything humanly possible for our children so that someday they can strut confidently into the real world. And we do it all in the name of love. But love can get us in trouble—not love itself, but how we show it. Our noble intentions can be our worst enemy when it comes to raising responsible kids.

Contrary to popular opinion, many of the most disrespectful, rebellious kids come from homes where they are shown love; it's just the wrong kind of love.

Ineffective Parenting Styles

Helicopter Parents

Some parents think love means living lives that revolve around their children. These are helicopter parents. Foster Cline and Jim Fay originated this widely used term to describe parents who hover over their children and rescue them when trouble arises. They're forever running lunches, permission slips, band instruments, and homework assignments to school. They're always pulling their children out of jams. Not a day goes by when they're not protecting little junior from something—usually a growing experience—he needs or deserves. As soon as their children send up an SOS flare, helicopter parents, already hovering nearby, swoop in and shield the children from teachers, playmates, and other apparently hostile elements.

While today these "loving" parents may feel they are easing their children's path into adulthood, tomorrow the same children will be leaving home and wasting the first eighteen months of their adult life flunking out of college or meandering about, "getting their heads together." Such children are unequipped for the challenges of life. Significant learning opportunities were stolen from them in the name of love.

In their zeal to protect their young, some helicopter parents swoop down like Apache attack helicopters on any person or agency they see as a threat to their child's impeccable credentials. Armed with verbal smart bombs, they are quick to blast away at anyone who sets high standards for behavior, morality, or achievement.

The irony is that people often view helicopter parents as model parents. They feel uncomfortable imposing consequences. When they see their children hurting, they hurt too, so they bail them out.

But the real world does not run on the bailout principle. Traffic tickets, overdue bills, irresponsible people, crippling diseases, taxes — these and other normal events of adult life usually do not disappear because a loving benefactor bails us out. Helicopter parents fail to prepare their kids to meet that kind of world.

The company who hires a helicopter kid won't be intimidated by parental pressure in the face of substandard performance. A perfect image and spotless school transcript are poor substitutes for character and the attitude that achievement comes through struggle and perseverance.

Aggressive protection of their children will accomplish the exact opposite of what helicopter parents are trying to achieve.

Drill Sergeant Parents

Other parents are like drill sergeants. They, too, love their children, but feel that the more they bark and the more they control, the better their kids will be in the long run. "These kids will be disciplined," the drill sergeant says. "They'll know how to act right." Indeed, they are constantly *told* what to do.

When drill sergeant parents talk to children, their words are often filled with put-downs and I-told-you-sos. These parents are into power! If children don't do what they're told, drill sergeant parents are going to—doggone it all—*make* them do it.

Kids of drill sergeant parents, when given the chance to think for themselves, often make horrendous decisions—to the complete consternation and disappointment of their parents. But it makes sense. These kids are rookies in the world of decision making. They've never had to think—the drill sergeant took care of that. The kids have been ordered around all their lives.

They're as dependent on their parents as the kids of helicopter parents are.

In addition, when children of drill sergeant parents reach their teen years, they are even more susceptible to peer pressure than most other teens. Why? Because as children, when the cost of mistakes was low, they were never allowed to make their own decisions but were trained to listen to a voice outside of their heads — that of their parents. When they reach their teen years and no longer want to listen to their parents, they still follow the same pattern, only this time the voice outside of their heads no longer belongs to their parents; it belongs to their friends. Drill sergeant parents tend to create kids who are followers because they have never learned how to make decisions for themselves.

Parents send messages to their children about what they think their kids are capable of. The message the helicopter parent sends is, "You are fragile and can't make it without me." The drill sergeant's message is, "You can't think for yourself, so I'll do it for you." While both of these parental types may successfully control their children in the early years, they will have done their kids a disservice once puberty is reached.

Helicopter children become adolescents unable to cope with outside forces, think for themselves, or handle their own problems. Drill sergeant kids, who did a lot of saluting when they were young, will do a lot of saluting when teenagers, but the salute is different: a raised fist or a crude gesture involving the middle finger.

The Effective Parenting Style of Love and Logic

The Consultant Parent

Helicopters can't hover forever, and eventually drill sergeants go hoarse. Allow us to introduce an alternative employed by Love and Logic parents that works well throughout life. While especially effective with teenagers, this style also reflects the attitude parents should have from the time their children are toddlers. We call it the consultant parenting style.

In their teens, children move from being concrete thinkers to being abstract thinkers. They need thoughtful guidance and firm, enforceable limits. We set those limits based on the safety of the child and how the child's behavior affects others. Then we maintain those limits to help children understand they are responsible for their actions and will suffer reasonable consequences for inappropriate actions. However, while parents are setting and holding these limits, it is important for them to continue encouraging their children to think about their behavior and to help them feel in control of their actions by giving choices within the limits. This is where the consultant parent comes in.

As our children grow into adolescents, this parenting style becomes even more important. Teens often resent guidelines and rebel at firm limits because they've grown to think differently than when they were younger. Because of this important change in cognition, parents must adjust the way they parent to meet the needs of the new thought processes of their adolescents. They step back a bit from being the enforcers of limits and let reasonable, real-world consequences do the teaching. They become advisors and counselors more than police officers, allowing their adolescents to make more decisions for themselves, and then guiding them to successfully navigate the consequences of those decisions.[2]

Love and Logic parents avoid the helicopter and drill sergeant mentalities by using a consultant style of parenting as early as possible in the child's life. They ask their children questions and offer choices. Instead of telling their children what to do, they put the burden of decision making on their kids' shoulders. They establish options within limits. Thus, by the time the children become teens, they are used to making good decisions.

To Protect Them Is Not to Love Them

America needs kids who can handle tough times, especially in this post-9/11, post–Hurricane Katrina world. Many of the issues Americans face in our schools and cities relate to acts of nature or terrorism, but our homes provide many coping opportunities. Generally, children take their cue on how to deal with challenges from adults in the environment they share. Learning how to handle small things—especially to fail at small things and grow through that affordable experience—is the best way to prepare our children for whatever they may face in the future.

Too many parents confuse *love*, *protection*, and *caring*. These concepts are not synonymous. Parents may refuse to allow their children to fail because they see such a response as uncaring.

Thus, they overcompensate with worry and hyperconcern.

What these parents are doing, in reality, is meeting their own selfish needs. They make more work for themselves and will, in the long run, raise children who make their own lives more work. *Protection* is not synonymous with *caring*, but both are a part of love.

Let's look at the way God operates. If we ask ourselves, "Does God care about us?" we'd probably respond, "Sure, God cares a lot about us." But if we then ask ourselves, "Would He let us jump off a cliff tonight?" we'd all have to admit, "Yeah, now that you mention it, He probably would." So does He *care*? Of course! Yet God loves without being overly protective.

Caring for our children does not equate to protecting them from every possible misstep they could make in growing up. Of course, when their child is an infant, responsible parents must respond to him with total protectiveness. Every problem an infant encounters really is the parents' problem. If parents do not protect an infant, he will die.

However, as children grow—beginning at about nine months of age with very simple choices—parents must make a gentle, gradual transition to allowing children the privilege of solving their own problems. By the time children are eleven or twelve years old, they should be able to make most decisions without parental input. Actually, to be truthful, parental love and attitude determine how children will handle most problems through early adolescence.

For instance, think about a group of mothers watching their toddlers wobble onto the ice during their first time on skates. Once the toddlers make their first inevitable crash on the ice, one group of moms, worried to death at the side of the rink, yells, "Are you hurt?" And the toddlers, scrunching up their faces and sliding back toward Mom, say in that distinctive toddler way, "Yeah, come to think of it, I *am* hurt." The other group of moms merely shouts, "Kaboom!" when the children go down, and their youngsters pick themselves up, dust off their bottoms, and go on skating, often saying, "Yeah, kaboom!" in agreement.

The first group of children learns that a fall is a painful experience. The second group learns from their mistakes, not concentrating on the pain and parental rescue. The problem is, rescuing parents often rescue out of their own needs. They like to heal hurts. They are parents who need to be needed, not parents who want to be wanted.

Children who have been shown love primarily through protection may be irreparably damaged by the time they reach high school. Parents of middle or high school children who must concern themselves with clothing, television habits, homework, teeth brushing, haircuts, and the like have at-risk children on their hands. At the very least, these children are not going to be much fun for their future spouse.

The challenge of parenting is to love kids enough to allow them to fail—to stand back, however painful it may be, and let significant learning opportunities (SLOs) build our children.

Responsibility Cannot Be Taught

Parents are forever moaning about their children's inability to absorb parental words of wisdom. It seems we can tell daughter Kayla a hundred times not to forget something, and sure enough, she walks out the door without it. We tell son Ryan to show some respect, and he answers, "Why do I have to do that? You're living in the Dark Ages!"

One thing for sure: We can't tell kids, "Be responsible." It doesn't work. Have you ever noticed that the parents who yell the loudest about responsibility seem to have the most irresponsible kids? The most responsible children usually come from families in which parents almost never use the word *responsibility*. It's a fact: Responsibility cannot be taught; it must be caught.

To help our children gain responsibility, we must offer them opportunities to be responsible. That's the key. Parents who raise responsible kids spend very little time and energy worrying about their kids' responsibilities; they worry more about how to let the children encounter SLOs for their *irresponsibility*. Certainly they are involved with their kids, lovingly using good judgment as to when their children are ready to learn the next level of life's lessons. But they don't spend their time reminding them or worrying for them. In a subtle way, they're saying, "I'm sure you'll remember on your own, but if you don't, you'll learn something from the experience." These parents are sympathetic but don't solve their kids' problems; they help their children understand they can solve their own problems.

Children who grow in responsibility also grow in self-esteem, a prerequisite for achievement in the real world. As their self-esteem and self-confidence grow, children are better able to make it once parental ties are cut.[3]

Responsible Children Feel Good about Themselves

Even children make themselves known by
their acts,
by whether what they do is pure and right.

PROVERBS 20:11

There are two types of kids in this world. One type gets up in the morning, looks in the mirror, and says, "Hey, look at that dude. He's all right! I like that guy, and I bet other people will like him too." The other type, when he looks in the mirror, says, "Oh, no, look at that boy. I really don't like what I see, and I bet other people won't like him either."

Two radically different outlooks on life; two radically different self-concepts. Children with a poor self-concept often forget to do homework, bully other kids, argue with teachers and parents, steal, and withdraw into themselves when things get rocky — they are irresponsible in all they do. Children with a good self-concept tend to have a lot of friends, do their chores regularly, and don't get into trouble in school — they take responsibility in their daily lives as a matter of course. Although this may seem simplistic, there is a direct correlation between self-concept and performance in school, at home, on the playground, or wherever children may be. Kids learn best and are responsible when they feel good about themselves.

When parenting with Love and Logic, we strive to offer our children a chance to develop that needed positive self-concept. With love enough to allow the children to fail, with love enough to allow the consequences of their actions to teach them about responsibility, and with love enough to help them celebrate the triumphs, our children's self-concept will grow each time they survive on their own.

I Am What I Think You Think I Am

Unfortunately, many parents don't give their children a chance to build a positive self-concept; instead, they concentrate on their children's weaknesses. They reason (often unknowingly), "Before my Elizabeth can be motivated to learn anything, she has to know how weak she is." Whenever these parents talk to their children, the conversation centers on what the children are doing poorly or what they can't do. If a child has trouble with fractions or has sloppy work habits or doesn't pronounce syllables properly—whatever the problem—the parents let him or her know about these weaknesses continually. The result is a constant eroding of their child's self-concept. But parents who build on their kids' strengths find their children growing in responsibility almost daily.

Think of how we, as adults, respond to a person who builds on our strengths. If somebody important to us thinks we're the greatest thing since the remote control, we will perform like gangbusters for that person. But if that important person thinks we're the scum of the earth, we will probably never prove him wrong.

It's the same way with kids. Kids say to themselves, *I don't become what* you think *I can, and I don't become what* I think *I can. I become what* I think you think *I can*. Then they spend most of their emotional energy looking for proof that what they think is our perception of them is correct. For example, long before Jim's son, Charlie, developed his writing skills, his seventh-grade teacher raved about his writing potential, building him up and encouraging him. Responding to what his teacher thought he could do, Charlie worked on his writing with determination and enthusiasm and is now an accomplished psychologist, public speaker, and author of several books.

As parents, we play an integral part in the building of a positive self-concept in our children. The messages we give our kids through our words and actions, in how we encourage and how we model, shape the way they feel about themselves. Unfortunately, many of the really powerful messages we send our children have covert negative meanings. We may mean well, but sometimes the words we use and the way we phrase them are received by our children as something totally different from what we meant to say. This is one of the tragedies of parent-child relationships.

For example, a simple question such as, "What are you doing that for?" packs a double meaning. The overt message seems like a simple question. However, what our child hears underneath is, "You're not very competent."

Such implied messages are put-downs, the kind of messages that would make us fighting mad if they were said to us by a supervisor or coworker. We can lace these messages with as much syrup as the human voice is capable of carrying—"Now honey, you're not going without your coat today, are you?"—but the implied message still shines through; namely, "You're not smart enough to know whether or not your own body is hot or cold." The ultimate implied message says, "I'm bigger than you are. I'm more powerful than you are. I have more authority, and I can make you do things."

Whenever we order our children to "Shut up!" or "Stop arguing!" or "Turn off the television!" we're sending a message that slashes into their self-concept. Why is this? Because when we give children orders, we are saying:

- "You don't take suggestions."
- "You can't figure out the answer for yourself."
- "You have to be told what to do by a voice outside your head."

Conversely, when we parent with Love and Logic, we emphasize a powerful combination: letting our children fail in nonthreatening situations while emphasizing their strengths. We must be uncritical and unprotective. Parents who raise irresponsible children do exactly the opposite! They're critical *and* protective.

Tip #1:
What We Say Is Not Always What Kids Hear

Kids are quick to understand the underlying messages we give, whether they come through words or actions. Each of the following examples carries both an overt and a covert meaning:

"Isabella, I'll let you decide that for yourself."
OVERT MESSAGE: "You can decide."
COVERT MESSAGE: "You are capable."

"Trevor, I'll give you one more chance, but you better shape up."
OVERT MESSAGE: "Things better improve."
COVERT MESSAGE: "You can't handle it. I have to provide another chance."

"Don't go out without your coat, Tessa."

OVERT MESSAGE: A simple reminder.

COVERT MESSAGE: "You're not capable of thinking for yourself."

Positive Self-Esteem Comes from Accomplishment

Kids get the most out of what they accomplish for themselves. Children will get more out of making their own decision—even if it is wrong—than they will out of parents making that decision for them. Sometimes that means standing by as our kids struggle to complete a task we could easily help them with or do for them.

It is normal for parents to want their children to have nice things and not have to struggle as much as they did growing up. However, that does not mean that because parents have the money (or, unfortunately, the credit limit) to buy their children whatever they want, they should buy it for them, nor does it mean that if they have the clout to get their kids out of a tough spot, they should do so. If we never let our kids struggle to get something they want or work through a problem for themselves, then when things get difficult later in life, they won't suddenly turn tough and get going; instead, they'll just quit. Ultimately, believing in themselves as capable human beings comes from accomplishing difficult things, not having those things done for them or being repeatedly told they are great kids.

Beyond our encouraging words, the pattern for building self-esteem and self-confidence looks something like this in almost every case:

1. Kids take a risk and try to do something they think they can't.
2. They struggle in the process of trying to do it.
3. After a time, they accomplish what they first set out to do.
4. They get the opportunity to reflect back on their accomplishment and can say, "Look at what I did!"

The final steps of forming a positive self-concept are an inside job—something kids have to do for themselves, by working hard and accomplishing good things. No amount of stuff or praise can build a resilient self-image for a child. Oddly enough, kids don't feel good about themselves when we do everything we can to keep them happy or give them everything they want. They have to sweat a little and earn things for themselves.

Of course, if we let them risk accomplishing difficult things, it means they might just as easily fail as succeed. They must know we love them whether they succeed or not, and we can support and encourage them along the way as long as we don't take their efforts away from them. By letting our kids work their way through age-appropriate tough times when they are younger, we are preparing them to effectively face truly tough times down the road.

Again, this must be done with common sense. We don't need to artificially create difficult situations for them, nor do we let them struggle with things too far beyond their abilities. For a toddler, building a block tower can be equivalent to a twelve-year-old learning to play a moderately difficult piece of music on the piano, but the reverse situation would be ridiculous. Love and Logic parents prepare and know how to keep the work and decision making in their kids' court rather than their own.

If We're Happy, They're Happy

You may find this an extremely distressing thought, but kids learn nearly every interpersonal activity by modeling. And you know who their primary models are, don't you? The way they handle fighting, frustration, problem solving, getting along with others, language, posture, movements—everything is learned by watching the big people in their lives. Their all-seeing eyes are scoping out our actions, from learning to talk to learning to drive.

By the time children are toilet trained, they're dressing up in Mom's shoes or wearing Dad's hat. If Mom's at the sink doing dishes, there they are too, splashing around and getting soaked. If Dad's under the hood tinkering with the carburetor, there the kids are, lending their "helping" hand. Many parents get irritated and feel it's a bother having the kids underfoot. But what learning opportunities—at low price tags! The key to parental modeling may sound strange to you, but it goes like this: I always model responsible, healthy adult behavior by taking good care of myself. The maxim of taking good care of ourselves — even putting ourselves first — may go against our parental grain. Many parents believe their kids should always come first. No sacrifice is too great. These parents are taxi driver, delivery service, alarm clock, travel agent, and financial analyst — all at the same time. However, children growing up with this arrangement see that their parents are not taking care of themselves in a healthy way. They're always putting the children first and themselves last. The kids will then model this behavior by putting themselves last as well.

When high school rolls around, these same parents will wonder why their children have such a poor self-image. After all, the parents say, "I always put them first. I always did everything for them." In reality, young people with a poor self-image are following their parental model. In the same self-depriving way, they're putting themselves last.

Of course, as parents we never put ourselves first at the expense of our children. We don't want them to lose out. We want them to win, but we should want to win as well. Thus, we always strive for a win-win situation. We want to feel good, and we want our children to feel good, so we model taking care of ourselves in a healthy way.

We still take our children places. We do things for them. But healthy people generally desire a two-way street—a situation where *both* parties win. So we enjoy taking our daughter to her soccer game not only because she enjoys it but also because we enjoy being with her and giving her the chance to excel. We like taking our son to his music lesson because we feel great watching his progress, chatting with him in the car, and generally enhancing the life he happily reflects back to us.

For many unhappy parents and their entitled, demanding children, life becomes a one-way street. The parent does things for the child, but the child feels no need to repay the parent or make the trips pleasant for the adult. The child only takes, and the parent only gives. Wise parents set the model by taking good care of themselves. A Love and Logic parent might say, "Honey, I know you want me to (help you with your homework; take you to your practice; drive you to the movie). However, I'm sorry to say that taking you places (doing things for you) has put a darkening cloud over my haze of happiness lately. That's sad but true. So I think I'll pass on doing it this time." This parent will raise respectful, thoughtful children who grow to take good care of themselves too.[4]

Tip #2: What They See Is What They Learn

I (Jim) spent my childhood on the wrong side of the tracks in a trailer in industrial Denver. When my family scraped enough money together, we bought a little garage to live in while my dad built a house on the property.

Dad worked a morning shift downtown, then when he returned at two p.m. every day, he picked up his hammer and saw and built a house. It took seven years.

At the end of the day, when my dad knocked off, he invariably said, "Jim, clean up this mess." So I would roll out the wheelbarrow, pick up a shovel and a rake, and clean up the mess. At the same time, Dad would explain to me that people have to learn to clean up after themselves. They need to finish and put the tools away.

When my dad noticed that I left my own stuff lying around, he complained, "Why don't you ever pick up your stuff, Jim? There's your bike on the sidewalk, and your tools are all over the place. When you go to look for a tool, you won't know where it is." I, of course, was learning all about cleaning up. I was learning that adults *don't* clean up after themselves.

Had my father modeled cleaning up after himself—saying in the process, "I feel good now that the day's work is finished, but I'll feel better when I clean up this mess and put all the tools in the right places"—he may have developed a son who liked to clean up his own messes. As it is, my garage is a mess to this very day.

Children's Mistakes Are Their Opportunities

How much better to get wisdom than gold!
To get understanding is
to be chosen rather than silver.

PROVERBS 16:16

Oftentimes we impede our kids' growth. We put ourselves exactly where we shouldn't be: in the middle of their problems. Parents who take on their kids' problems do them a great disservice. They rob their children of the chance to grow in responsibility, and they actually foster further irresponsible behavior.

The greatest gift we can give our children is the knowledge that with God's help, they can always look first to themselves for the answers to their problems. Kids who develop an attitude that says *I can probably find my own solutions* become survivors. They have an edge in learning, relating to others, and making their way in the world. That's because the best solution to any problem lies within the skin of the person who owns the problem.

When we solve problems for our kids — the ones they could handle on their own — they're never quite satisfied. Our solution is never quite good enough. When we tell our kids what to do, deep down they say, *I can think for myself,* so oftentimes they do the exact opposite of what we want them to do.

Kids who deal directly with their own problems are moved to solve them. They know that if they don't, nobody will. Not their parents, not their teachers — nobody. And on a subconscious level, they feel much better about themselves when they handle their own problems.

You Have Your Troubles, I Have Mine

The list of kids' problems is endless: getting to school on time, getting to school at all, being hassled by friends, hassling friends, harassing teachers, being harassed by teachers, poor grades, laziness, wrong choice of friends, drugs, alcohol, and many, many more. Parents who involve themselves in all these problems can spend their every waking hour at the task. Unfortunately, these parents believe they are showing love for their children by jumping into conflicts and rescuing them.

Tip #3: When to Step In/ When to Stay Out of Kids' Problems

Occasionally, we should make our children's problems our problems:

- We step in when our children are in definite danger of losing life or limb or of making a decision that could affect them for a lifetime.
- We step in when our children know they are in a situation they can't handle by themselves. More important, perhaps, is that they know *we* also know they can't handle it. So when we step in and help them out—saying in essence, "You are incapable of coping with this situation"—it is not a destructive message, because everyone is aware of the child's inability to handle the situation.

Remember: Everything we fix for our kids, our kids will be unable to fix for themselves. If there's more than a 20 percent chance our child might be able to work it out, we should keep clear of owning the problem and not rob our child of the opportunity to learn and grow from the experience.

Even when a kid doesn't seem concerned about his or her problems, we should stay out of them. A child's laziness, for example, is still a child's problem. While untouched homework, bad grades, or tardiness at school may be maddening to us, we must find a loving way to allow the consequences to do the teaching for the child, whatever those consequences might be.

On the other hand, some of the child's behaviors *are* our problems. If the problem is how our children relate to us (disrespectful talk, sassing, rude gestures or behavior), how they do chores, playing loud music, waking us up in the middle of the night, misbehaving when in public, or matters surrounding their life support system (bread and butter, room and board), then the problem has drifted out of their domain and directly into ours. In short, if it's a problem for us, it should soon be a problem for them.

If Connor shoots off his mouth at school, we

let the teachers take care of the consequences with our support. But if Connor shoots his mouth off at us, we deal with it.

If Mariah's slowness in getting ready for school makes her late, we stay clear of the problem. But if Mariah's slowness in getting ready to leave the house makes *us* late, we deal with it.

If Caden's room is a disaster area, we let him wallow in the mire. But if Caden trashes the living room within fifteen seconds of arrival, that affects us, so we help him handle it—our way.

Again, we are modeling appropriate adult behavior. We don't allow other people to harm us, and therefore we raise children who know how to care for themselves and won't allow others to cause them problems.

The Two Rules of Love and Logic

Over the years, we have used two principles to guide what we wanted Love and Logic to be: the first was that it had to be as effective as possible, and the second was that we wanted to keep it as simple as possible so that parents could remember it even in the midst of highly emotional times. Because of this, we have summarized the Love and Logic method in two simple rules that will help you do all that we have discussed so far:

1. Adults must set firm, loving limits using enforceable statements without showing anger, lecturing, or using threats. The statements are enforceable because they deal with how we will respond.
2. When a child causes a problem, the adult shows empathy through sadness and sorrow and then lovingly hands the problem and its consequences back to the child.

It is crucial to understand these two rules as the foundation for all that Love and Logic has to offer you. Because of this, it is worth taking time here to explore them in more detail.

Adults must set firm, loving limits using enforceable statements without showing anger, lecturing, or using threats.

Perhaps the most important skill from this first rule is the use of enforceable statements. Often, this is best done by giving choices that are within your firm, loving limits. For example, if a toddler is acting inappropriately, the parent can sing the "Uh-Oh" song and give him a choice: "Would you like to go to your room walking, or would you like me to carry you?" The limit in this case is that the child cannot act as he just did in the parent's presence and that the best place for the child to be, then, is in his room.

Notice that the parent is not telling the child how to act, such as "Stop that right now!" Such a statement is not enforceable; all it means is that the parent will have to act again if the behavior continues. Nor does the parent simply say, "Go to your room," because that also gives the child the option of disobedience. Instead, two choices are given, both of which are acceptable to the parent and can be enforced if the child decides to do nothing in response. It also shares some modicum of control with the child, and any consequences come from the child's decision, not the parent's.

For example, let's say the child continues to misbehave in response to the question "Would you like to go to your room walking, or would you like me to carry you?" Then the parent can again say, "Uh-oh! It looks as if you chose being carried." Then when the parent deposits the child in the room, the parent can up the ante a bit and show who is really in control of the situation: "Here we are in your room. Feel free to continue your tantrum here if you would like. Would you like to stay in your room with the door open or closed?" If the child decides to flee out the door at that point, then the response is, "Uh-oh! Looks like you chose to be in here with the door shut."

Of course, few kids will stop here. A shut door is easily opened again. Then again, when the parent shuts the door, another choice can be given: "Would you like the door just to be shut, or would you like it to be shut and locked? Then I will see you when you are sweet again."

Now, we don't advocate locking children in their rooms and abandoning them there—such actions are tantamount to child abuse. However, if the parent will stay nearby and watchful, she will not have to do this too many times before the child simply chooses to have the door shut without testing it again. If the parent locks the child in the room, she should stay nearby, wait until the tantrum inside has finished, give it a minute or so, and then open the door. We advocate then saying something along the line of, "Oh, I missed you! I am glad to see you are feeling sweeter! Let me set this egg timer to five minutes, and you can come out to be with me again when it goes off if you will stay sweet that whole time."

It is not uncommon after a few interactions like this that the more drastic actions don't have to happen. In fact, many children who grow used to this will hear the "Uh-Oh" song and head toward their rooms without anything else being said.

Of course, the younger the child is when you start using enforceable statements, the easier it is later in life. Here are a few examples:

- "Please feel free to join us for dinner when your room is clean."
- "Would you prefer to wear something nice to church or go in your pajamas?"
- "Feel free to join us in the living room to watch some television once your chores are finished."
- "You are free to use the car as long as your mother or I don't need it, once you have deposited the insurance deductible in a savings account, and as long as I don't have to worry about alcohol or drugs."

While some of these can cause some embarrassing situations (no one really wants to take their kids to church in their pajamas), none of them is dangerous or unenforceable. Certainly, a toddler showing up for church in his pajamas is better than a grade-schooler doing the same, but neither is outlandish.

Make sure you are willing to enforce whatever choices you give. It won't take too many times of following through on the less desirable choice before your child will understand that either option is truly acceptable to you and that you will carry it out.

By contrast, stay away from alternatives both you and your child know you won't carry out. We would love to have a dollar for every time we have heard a parent at a fast-food restaurant say, "Hurry up and eat, or I am just going to leave you here!" Both the anger in the comment and the outlandishness of the options let everyone in earshot know who really is in control of that situation, and the child is more likely to continue racing his fries around his burger than put anything into his or her mouth.

When a child causes a problem, the adult shows empathy through sadness and sorrow and then lovingly hands the problem and its consequences back to the child.

One of the points of the "Uh-Oh" song is for the parent to show sadness at the actions of their child. Singing the "Uh-Oh" song is another way of saying, "Oh, what a sad choice you just made." For older kids, this can change to something along the lines of "Bummer" or "Oh, how sad. That never turns out very well for me when I do that," or something else along those lines. The truth of the matter is that consultant parents tend to have very limited vocabularies and respond with the same phrases over and over throughout their children's lives, locking in the fact that parents love them and feel sad when they make the wrong choices. This reinforces that the parent will not take ownership of the problems or consequences caused by their children's bad choices but will gladly love them through solving those problems for themselves and dealing with those consequences.

Two other points beneath this rule are also crucial to understand here. The first is that the most important thing for consultant parents to learn, especially if their children are older, is to neutralize their child's arguing. A parent can do a beautiful job of setting firm limits with an enforceable statement, showing empathy at their child's mistake, and turning the problem back over to the child, and then completely destroy anything positive the child can learn from the interaction by getting dragged into an argument with their kid. Consultant parents blow in, blow off, and then blow out—they don't blow up!

Our best advice for parents who have reached the blowing-up point is to go completely mindless and return to their one-liners. Some of the best are, "I love you too much to argue with you," "I know," and "Nice try!" The conversation could go something like this:

> JESSICA: "But Dad, that's not fair!"
> DAD: "I know."
> JESSICA: "But none of my friends
>   would have to do anything like that!"
> DAD: "I know."
> JESSICA: "If that is the way you feel,
>   then you just don't love me!"
> DAD: "Nice try! You know I will love
>   you no matter what happens."

JESSICA: "Ugh! I can't talk to you! You are so five-minutes-ago! None of my friends has a parent like you!"

DAD: "I know, it must be a bummer to have a father like me sometimes, but you know what? I love you too much to argue with you. We should discuss this when both of us are less emotional about it."

The second point is that consequences can, and often should, be delayed. There is nothing wrong with saying something like, "Uh-oh! I am going to have to do something about that, but not right now. I am busy with something else. I will get back to you on that. Try not to worry about it." This is especially good if you are in the car and truly can't do anything about it at the moment, if you are out in public, or if you simply can't think of anything to do about it. It is okay to take some time and call a friend, teacher, advisor, or minister to get some good ideas about how to respond. Perhaps you could return to this book or check our Love and Logic website at www .loveandlogic.com for ideas.

Many people have been taught that the best

time to respond is immediately because the impact will be lost if time passes. But haven't you ever experienced a two-year-old remembering a promise made a week ago about getting something she wanted the next time Mommy took her to the store? Don't worry! Your kids have a good memory too. And often in the time between problem and consequence, either they'll find a solution to the problem for themselves or the perfect consequence will present itself to you so that the children will get optimal learning out of the situation!

The key is to keep the ball in the kids' court and model taking care of yourself. Then, even if the kids think they have gotten away with it, when consequences come they will be more meaningful because you took the time to find the best response.[5]

It's Never Too Late to Start

Even if our kids are in their teens and have never been exposed to Love and Logic discipline, they—and we—can benefit from our putting it to use. The important thing is to build a relationship with our kids that will last a lifetime, long past their adolescent years. And it is never too late to work on that.[6]

Our children are our most precious resource. They come to us with one request: "During our short eighteen years with you, please teach us the truth about life and prepare us to be responsible adults when we leave home and enter the real world." In the course of those eighteen years, we'll be faced with many challenges in parenting. Our love will be on the line every time they have a problem. That love has the potential to be either ally or enemy—to either help our children learn what they need to know, or to prevent them from growing to be responsible adults.

Let's grant our kids' request. Let's love them enough to allow them to learn the necessary and crucial skill of responsible thinking and living.[7]

Notes

1. "Parenting: Joy or Nightmare?" is excerpted and adapted from Foster Cline, MD, and Jim Fay, *Parenting with Love and Logic: Teaching Children Responsibility* (Colorado Springs, CO: NavPress, 2006), 17–20.
2. For more on being a consultant parent to adolescents, see our book *Parenting Teens with Love and Logic*.
3. "Mission Possible: Raising Responsible Kids" is excerpted and adapted from *Parenting with Love and Logic*, 21–27, 32–34.
4. "Responsible Children Feel Good about Themselves" is excerpted and adapted from *Parenting with Love and Logic*, 35–38, 46–50.
5. "Children's Mistakes Are Their Opportunities" is excerpted and adapted from *Parenting with Love and Logic*, 51–61.
6. "It's Never Too Late to Start" is excerpted from *Parenting with Love and Logic*, 116.
7. The content for *Parenting Without the Power Struggles* has been excerpted from portions of chapters 1–4 and 8 of *Parenting with Love and Logic*. You can find the full chapters and Love and Logic philosophy, as well as forty-eight Love and Logic parenting tools, in the updated and expanded edition of Foster Cline, MD, and Jim Fay, *Parenting with Love and Logic: Teaching Children Responsibility* (Colorado Springs, CO: NavPress, 2006).

About the Authors

Foster Cline, MD, is an internationally recognized psychiatrist. He is a consultant to mental health organizations, parent groups, and schools across North America. He specializes in working with difficult children.

Jim Fay has thirty-one years of experience as an educator and school principal. He is recognized as one of America's top educational consultants and has received many awards in the educational field. He has successfully guided his three children through their childhood and teen years using love and logic.

For more information, go to www.loveand logic.com.

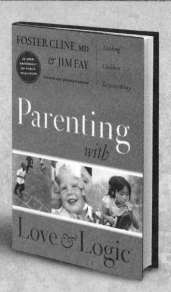